SIMPLIFY
YOUR LIFE

SIMPLIFY
YOUR LIFE

8 SIMPLE PRINCIPLES TO TURN YOUR CHAOS INTO CALM

ANDREA BRUNDAGE, MBA

Gold Canyon Press • Gold Canyon, Arizona • 2019

First Edition

Copyright © 2019 by Andrea Brundage

Gold Canyon Press

Published in the United States by
GOLD CANYON PRESS
Gold Canyon, Arizona

Cover image by Andrea Brundage
Cover design by Yolie Hernandez, AZ Book Designer

ISBN 978-1-7336758-0-2 (Print)
ISBN 978-1-7336758-1-9 (e-Book)

Printed in the United States of America

This book is dedicated to those who
struggle with overwhelm created by clutter,
chaos, and having too much stuff.

There is hope,
I promise.

NOTE TO THE READER

THE GOAL OF THIS BOOK is to provide encouragement and to address as many scenarios as possible. If your particular situation is not covered, it was not to exclude you; it was simply an oversight.

The suggestions and instructions offered in this book are for informational purposes only and are not intended as a substitute for competent counselors, medical professionals, or attorneys.

Any comments or questions should be directed to
info@AndreaBrundage.com

CONTENTS

ACKNOWLEDGEMENTS

I HONOR MY MOTHER COLLEEN, who was a young girl during the depression era and was deeply affected by the sense of lack. The hard times she lived through as a young, impressionable child contributed to her need to keep things that might be used some day. I didn't understand it then, but I do now. At 93-years old, she is still teaching me valuable lessons. Only now the lessons are about acceptance and grace.

A huge thank you to family and friends who encouraged me as I left the corporate world and started my own professional organizing business. Your support fuels me every day.

This book would not have happened had it not been for my trusting clients. Your willingness to be vulnerable and to ask for help is acknowledged and appreciated.

Thank you to my first readers. I appreciate your constructive, helpful, and kind input. Thank you Mallary Tytel, Ph.D., Alana Roberts, Sharyn Jordan Hathcock, Diane Elarde, Nancy Tossell, Donna Smallin Kuper, Paulette Ensign, and Scottie Jones.

Thank you to my final editors, Lesli Pintor and Elizabeth Kimmie Smith, and to my book designer, Yolie Hernandez of AZ Book Design. Your role in my journey has helped me create this tool for those who need it most.

Organization is a teachable skill.

INTRODUCTION

M Y HOPE IS THAT AS YOU ARE READING THIS BOOK, you will feel inspired, empowered, and better equipped to regain control over the clutter in your life. I also hope you will take steps to create a more simplified life for yourself. Organization is a teachable skill and you *can* learn how to be more organized.

What this book is about

- ► Helping you become more intentional about what you allow in your space and in your life.

- ► Giving you permission to let go of things that you no longer love, want, or use.

- ► Inspiring and empowering you.

- ► Making decisions.

- ► Offering tips and encouragement to support you as you tackle clutter, organize, and simplify your life.

- ► Recognizing personal tendencies that may be contributing to your cluttered spaces.

- ► Taking action!

What this book is not about

► Getting rid of everything you own.

► Living in a tiny house, nor is it about living off the grid.

► Being perfect.

Let me repeat, this book is not about being perfect.

What lies ahead?

The chapters that follow provide a framework with actionable steps and prompts to guide and encourage you through the process of turning your chaos into calm. You will have opportunities for self-reflection and quotes to inspire you along the journey.

The chapters in this book follow a simple approach to help you take action. My SIMPLIFY program is as follows:

Simplify your life

Identify problem areas

Make "me" time

Plan ahead

Let go of excess

Involve your people

Find help

You can do it!

By the time you finish this book, I hope you have made huge strides towards a simplified life. You may have more to do to get there, but if you stick with the principles outlined in the book you will be well on your way.

Distractions, Directions, Celebrations

Books can be a distraction if they keep you from moving into action. As you work your way through this book, I recommend you read a little and then get up and start a decluttering or organizing project.

Once you have made some progress, take a moment to acknowledge your hard work. Celebrating little victories can keep you moving forward, especially on days when you feel overwhelmed.

Start small. Think big.

You will see this phrase repeated in this book several times because it is so important. Getting organized is a process and is accomplished through intentional action. I will encourage you to work on projects that are realistic for the time you have available. The big picture will always be the end goal, but breaking large projects into smaller tasks will help you.

Simplicity is the ultimate sophistication.
- Leonardo da Vinci

1

SIMPLIFY YOUR LIFE

What does *simplifying* life mean anyway?

THE SHORT ANSWER IS, IT DEPENDS. For you, simplifying may mean having nothing in your space that does not add value. It may mean purging and organizing piles of mail and paperwork. To someone else it may mean purging closets of excess clothes, shoes, and accessories.

It could also mean making room in the garage for the car or cars. Or perhaps you are an empty-nester or retiree and you want to repurpose rooms in your home for your hobbies, or maybe you are ready to downsize, or what I like to refer to as *right-size*.

Simplifying life can relate to releasing commitments on your calendar. It can also mean allowing yourself time to plan ahead so you aren't constantly operating in react mode.

You may have many reasons why you want to simplify your life. You know better than anyone where you feel cluttered, overwhelmed, restless, and stuck. It is in those areas where simplifying life could be beneficial.

Current Trends

Being too busy and stressed is a way of life for many these days. People are running fast, working hard, and many are exhausted. It is not unusual for me to talk with young families who are running in a hundred different directions. They are so busy they rarely have time just to be home, to be still, and simply to enjoy each other's company.

One client of mine, a professional with a young family, shared that he and his partner *land* at home at night. He said their weekends typically consist of trying to tackle the never-ending list of projects, which leaves little room for family time and fun. Frustrated, he added, "Even when we are working together at home on a project, we never seem to get anything done...and then it's Monday again and off to work we go." After a heavy sigh he said, "We are overwhelmed, and we don't know where to start. Can you help us?"

Many working adults feel like they are on a hamster wheel, going through the motions, so to speak. Some admit they are too busy at work to take a day off, not to mention being unable to use up their accumulated vacation days. Are you too busy to take a day off to relax and have some fun?

Similarly, some retirees have accumulated so much stuff through the years that they, too, feel overwhelmed and stuck. A colleague of mine is a realtor who specializes in serving the senior community. She says many of her clients stay in homes that are too big for them because they simply can't face dealing with all the stuff. Their *golden years* are not feeling so golden to them.

In each of these scenarios, chaos is running the show. Lives are hijacked by too many activities, responsibilities at work, trying to balance work and life, and difficulty making decisions about what matters most.

Case Studies (names have been changed)

Whatever you're feeling, you're not alone. I have worked with hundreds of clients through the years, and each one has a different story and a different desired outcome. Yet, many of the stories describe similar feelings. Below are some examples of people whose stories may be similar to yours.

Kelley

Kelley is a successful business woman. She is respected in her community and amongst her peers. She refers to herself as an over-achiever and a perfectionist. Kelley always looks put together on the outside - polished and professional - but her home is a different story. Kelley had a little secret. Clutter had taken over her home and she couldn't stand to be there. She admitted she prefers to stay long hours at the office rather than go home to face the mess.

Her vision: Clear the clutter and turn her chaotic home into a calm and supportive space.

Missy

Missy has a home that looks tidy on the surface, but she is harboring a secret. Missy describes herself as a "drawer stuffer." Anything that is out of place gets shoved in a drawer, cabinet, closet, or put into the garage. In her case, opening a closet door could lead to a bump on the head, and the boxes in the garage made it impossible to park her car in there. Missy was embarrassed by her messy drawers and closets and she wanted to simplify her life.

Her vision: Everything has a place, and everything is in its place. Anything unwanted or unneeded is gone!

Angela

Angela panicked when her mother-in-law called to tell her she was dropping over in 10 minutes for a quick visit. She grabbed an empty box and did a quick swipe over her kitchen countertops, effectively dumping all the contents into the box.

The box was closed up and placed in the garage - and forgotten. Forgotten, that is, until we opened it during an organizing session many months later. Inside were what you might expect - bills, magazines, junk mail, expired coupons, etc. But that's not all we found.

We uncovered unused gift cards (same as cash), important paperwork that Angela had been looking for, and a piece of expensive jewelry that had gone missing. Angela almost broke down when we came across the stamped, addressed birthday card intended for her elderly mother. The envelope also contained a $50 check she had made out to her mom. Sadly, the card and check were never mailed, and Angela felt awful.

Her vision: A more orderly home that doesn't leave her frantic when someone unexpectedly drops over for a visit.

Mike

Mike was stressed and overwhelmed with the prospect of having to clean out and organize his messy garage without help. He didn't know where to begin, nor did he know what to do with the things he no longer wanted. I had previously helped this client and his wife with office and craft room organizing projects, so they gave me a call.

His vision: Tools and outdoor equipment organized and clearly labeled in built-in cabinets and on installed shelves. No unnecessary junk, and all items designated for donation loaded up and delivered to charity.

Ted

Ted is an airline pilot with a side business in the cruise industry. Ted's office was chaotic. He had a mix of business paperwork and his personal paperwork. Boxes on the floor were filled with mail, old marketing materials, accounting paperwork, receipts, etc. Ted's erratic schedule left him feeling overwhelmed and unfocused. He was considering hiring administrative support, but he knew he couldn't bring anyone in until he had some order to the chaos.

His vision: Organize the office and set up effective office systems so he could hire and train an assistant.

> The journey of a thousand miles
> begins with one step.
> - Lao Tzu

The journey begins

So here you are, and you are ready to take action, right? You are ready to simplify your life! You are ready to turn your chaos into calm.

Your journey to *Simplify Your Life* is about to begin. It's time to start thinking about what a simplified life looks like to you. Think about areas in your life where you feel cluttered and chaotic. Now imagine what those same areas will look and feel like when they are simplified and contain no clutter.

Everyone will have a different vision at this point. Maybe you just want to come home after a long day of work and feel at peace when you walk in the door. Or perhaps your vision is to get rid of everything and be a full-time RV'er. A young woman I recently met has a vision to live on a boat so she can sail full-time. You decide what motivates you.

This is *your* vision and this vision will be your focal point as you work through the following chapters. You may have several visions that come to mind, but let's keep it simple for now. Choose one to start.

If you aren't able to come up with a vision right this minute, don't worry. Keep reading and do the activities in the book that apply to you. When you complete the action steps, you will begin to see progress, and perhaps your vision will reveal itself to you.

Here's an idea

Do you have a friend, colleague, neighbor, or family member who wants to simplify life, too? Invite that person to join you on this journey. You can support each other, challenge each other, and celebrate each other's victories along the way.

Who do you know that would like to take the *Simplify Your Life* journey with you? Jot their names and contact information here.

Call them now and let's get started!

_____

_____

_____

_____

_____

_____

_____

_____

_____

For additional support, join the *SOS Clutter Disruptors* Facebook group. This is a safe environment where you can share your successes and struggles. And remember to post Before & After photos of your projects so we can cheer you on!

How many of these statements describe you?

I'm so overwhelmed.

I'm stressed out.

I can't find anything I need.

My house is always a mess.

My desk looks like a bomb went off.

I wish I had more hours in the day.

I just want to run away.

I'd rather stay at work than be at home.

I'm too embarrassed to have people over.

I don't even know where to begin.

You may recognize yourself in one or several of these statements. The list simply puts words to how you may feel or what you might be going through. It's possible that how you feel and what you're going through isn't on the list. That's okay, too.

Review the list on the previous page.

What else are you feeling? Jot your answers here.

_____

_____

_____

_____

_____

_____

_____

_____

_____

_____

_____

_____

_____

_____

_____

_____

_____

Where to begin?

This is where your work begins. Let's get started!

Reflection

Reflection is an important first step because without a willingness to acknowledge how you got where you are, it will be difficult to know what changes to make to improve your current situation.

Recognizing there is an issue is the first step. Having a desire to change your current situation is next.

What follows is the *action* (work) phase, followed by a commitment to stick to it.

The goal is to create new habits that support a more simplified life.

► What habits and tendencies have contributed to the clutter and chaos in your home, your life?

► Have major events contributed to or complicated your life? If so, what are they?

► Could you have done anything to avoid those event(s)?

► What other factors could be contributing to the clutter and chaos?

► Can you change or control any of these factors?

► Are you willing and able to do the work it will take to simplify and get organized?

► Are you ready to begin this journey?

Once you are clear about how you got where you are and what, if any, factors have contributed, the next step is to get really clear about where you want to go.

What does a *simplified life* look like to you? Those images are powerful and translate into goals.

Exercise

Write down your goals for your simplified life. Don't get stuck here, please. Just take a few minutes and jot down some things that you want to work on as you go through the process of turning chaos into calm.

_____

_____

_____

_____

_____

_____

_____

_____

_____

Next

Give some thought to the steps needed for you to reach your goals. Timelines can be effective here. If timelines motivate you, write the target completion date next to each goal.

Look at you! You are already creating the blueprint for your simplified life!

Some thoughts on goals

Are your goals realistic? Are they achievable? If yes, move forward. If not, adjust expectations. Set yourself up for success.

Start small. Think big.

Just like a house is built in logical phases, you will want to work on projects that build upon each other. Start with smaller tasks, but always keep the big picture in mind.

Speaking of pictures, be sure to take photos of your projects before you begin and take them again once you have completed the project. These images can serve as inspiration on days when you feel stuck and unproductive.

Photographs memorialize where you started and how far you've come. You will be amazed at how inspirational those photos can be as you tackle larger, more complex projects.

Challenge — Do one thing now

Start by tackling one small project. Choose one project that you can start and finish in the time you have available. Here are some ideas for small projects.

- ► Clean out the junk drawer.

- ► Clean out the refrigerator.

- ► Make the bed.

- ► Clear out obsolete electronics and cords.

- ► Toss out/shred junk mail.

- ► Toss out expired coupons.

- ► Toss out receipts not needed for tax purposes, returns, or warranties.

- ► Clean out the interior of the car.

- ► Return something you borrowed.

Ready, Set, Go!

   Step 1 – Decide on your project.

   Step 2 – Take *Before* photos.

   Step 3 – Action! It's time to sort, purge, organize.

   Step 4 – Take *After* photos!

If you feel motivated to continue, return to Step 1 and start another project. If you decide to stop now, that's fine.

   Take a moment to celebrate your accomplishments and be sure to share those Before and After photos with someone who is supportive!

A goal is just a dream
if not followed by action.

Notes

The first step in solving a problem
is to recognize that it does exist.
- Zig Ziglar

2

IDENTIFY PROBLEM AREAS

According to Dictionary.com, the verb clutter means *to fill or litter with things in a disorderly manner*. Clutter is often a result of poor habits, inadequate life-flow systems, delayed decisions, and unconscious consumerism (overbuying).

Life flow and systems

Life flow is how you move through your home, and it starts at the door you enter.

If you walk in, kick off your shoes, drop your overcoat on the floor, toss the mail on the kitchen counter, then your life flow could use some organizational systems.

Here are examples of life flow systems that could simplify your life.

► Install a key holder on the wall where you enter your home and hang your keys there every day.

► Install hooks for backpacks, coats, purses, briefcases, etc. These hooks might be installed in a mud room, entry way or even a garage.

► If shoes tend to accumulate in the entry way or at the door where you enter, consider putting a shelf or bins just outside that entry point. Or better yet, get in the habit of taking your shoes all the way to your bedroom and putting them in your closet.

► Sort and process mail daily. Keep only what you need. Toss or shred outer envelopes and marketing inserts. Unfold the statements and place in a folder. That folder might be labeled, *To Do* or *To Pay* or *Follow Up Required*. Do this daily and you will no longer have a countertop cluttered with accumulated mail.

► Put your toothbrush and toothpaste away after each use.

► Put makeup and shaving products away every day.

Home

Each home has its own flow. But sometimes clutter can affect the entire home, or it may be contained to specific areas. Good habits and effective organizational systems will provide support as you simplify your life and turn your chaos into calm. Below are common problem areas in the home.

Kitchen cabinets and pantries

too many plastic containers

too many utensils

too many empty glass jars

expired food

rancid oil, nuts, crackers

multiples of foil, plastic wrap, sandwich bags

overabundance of canned goods

overabundance of boxed foods

surplus paper supplies

vitamins, supplements

protein and diet powders

old candy

party or holiday supplies

rarely used appliances (bread makers, etc.)

Refrigerators

old leftover containers from restaurants

moldy or spoiled food

wilted, spoiled vegetables

expired condiments

Closets

a mishmash of hanger styles

too many clothes for the space

too many shoes for the space

too many hats, ties, gloves

too much jewelry

too many purses

clothing on the floor

overflowing laundry baskets

shoes cluttering up the floor

extra bathroom supplies

shopping bags

empty boxes

dry cleaning bags

vitamins, supplements

sentimental items, heirlooms

luggage

gifts

Bathrooms

excess amount of beauty and shaving products

bottles, jars, and cans of hair care products

surplus paper supplies

towels, washcloths

Linen closets

extra towels, washcloths, sheets

surplus paper products

games, tools

Laundry rooms

    piles of laundry

    hanging clothes

    multiple laundry bins

    laundry supplies

    cleaning supplies

    old towels and cleaning rags

    sporting goods

    tools, light bulbs

    flashlights, batteries

Toys/Games

    too many toys and games

    stuffed animals

    books and magazines scattered around the room

    food, food containers, drinks

    blankets and pillows

    dirty clothes

    art supplies

    art projects

    balls, sporting goods

    broken things

Garages

> empty boxes, packaging

> broken items from inside the house

> shoes (from kicking them off at the door)

> clothes (uniforms, laundry)

> moving boxes that were never unpacked

> things set aside for donating

> old furniture, broken furniture

> other people's things

> family photos and heirlooms

> extra dishes, pans, etc.

> books

> sporting goods

> crafts, unfinished projects

> holiday décor

> tools

Office

Just like our homes, offices are often cluttered as well. The list below outlines several areas to consider.

Paper

> receipts

unopened mail

junk mail

unfiled paperwork and file folders

magazines

schoolwork

medical bills

important documents

books

Miscellaneous

crafts

office supplies

family photos, albums, negatives, slides, etc.

Filing cabinets and storage boxes

filled to capacity

outdated or obsolete paperwork

decades worth of tax returns

Electronic clutter

thousands of unopened emails

saved emails

multiple hard drives

outdated office and electronic equipment

old media such as cassette and VHS tapes

Overbuying

It's easy to overbuy when you don't know what you have. Overbuying often takes place at the grocery store and the big box stores. You think, *"It's on sale so I'll buy it,"* and then you buy three instead of one because *"It's such a good deal."* Or maybe you think, *"It's so much cheaper here. I'll just get it."*

And then you have to find a place for those 14 cans of beans or 24 rolls of toilet paper. And as you go to put them away you realize you bought beans and toilet paper last time you were shopping. Now you have to deal with 28 cans of beans and 48 rolls of toilet paper.

Emotional buying

Buying new things is, and should be, fun and exciting. But these purchases should be made consciously and for the right reasons.

Shopping in a highly emotional state can be a recipe for disaster. It is during those times that some tend to make rash decisions, overspend, overbuy, and create debt. Be careful about making purchases when you feel sad, emotional, distressed, desperate, frustrated, angry, resentful, or revengeful.

Recognize the difference between impulse buying and conscious or mindful buying. Whenever you shop, consider the impact the transaction will have on you, your finances, and your space.

Online shopping

Shopping online is convenient (and addicting). Buying something that only requires a click on a SUBMIT box creates a disconnect. If you tend to overspend, be careful with online shopping.

And do not fall for the *"People who purchased this also purchased this"* game. It's a ploy to get you to buy more! And when your purchase arrives, ignore those coupons they tuck inside the box.

Remember the saying "The road to bankruptcy is paved in good deals." Become a mindful consumer.

Before you checkout online, take a moment to ask yourself these questions.

Do I *need* this or do I just *want* it?

Am I buying this just because it's a good deal?

Do I already have something similar?

Will it serve me well?

Can I really afford this?

Do I have room to store this?

Is there something else I would rather use this money for?

Challenge – It's clutter clearing time

Where are your problem areas?

What are three things you will do this week to clear some clutter from your home or office? This is a good time to remind you, *Start small. Think big.*

Steps to start

1. Evaluate how much time you have available for the project(s)

2. Choose a project you can start and complete in that time frame

3. Start

4. Finish

5. Celebrate

6. Return to Step 1

As you continue on this journey of simplifying your life, you will likely find that starting and finishing projects makes you feel accomplished and productive.

Celebrate those victories and let those good feelings create momentum. Observe how your confidence grows. Keep going! You have everything you need to tackle bigger projects.

Remember, organizing is not a one-and-done proposition. Once a space is organized, maintenance of that space is a requirement. Here's the best thing: If you happen to backslide and start to fall back into your old dysfunctional habits, you can start over!

STEPS	GOAL	COMPLETE BY

STEPS	GOAL	COMPLETE BY

STEPS	GOAL	COMPLETE BY

Project Checklist

What is your project?

How much time will you allocate to the project?

Take *Before* photos of your project now.

 Bookmark this page and then get to work. Come back to this page when you're finished with the project.

You did it! Good for you!

Take *After* photos of your project.

How do you feel when you look at the *Before* and *After* photos?

Getting organized is a project.
Staying organized is a lifestyle.

3

<u>M</u>AKE "ME" TIME

IF YOU WANT TO LIVE YOUR BEST LIFE - every day of your life – start with being more mindful of how you're allocating your time. Do you allow ample time for yourself to refresh and recharge, or do you just give to others and have nothing left for yourself?

Self-care is not selfish; in fact, it is quite the opposite. Would taking time to care for yourself make you feel happier? Could it also contribute to a healthier you? Making "me" time is something that can recharge your battery, rebuild your energy, fill your heart, and just make you feel better.

Wouldn't you agree being happier and healthier would feel great? If you felt happier, could you also positively impact everyone you come in contact with? How might a happier, healthier you affect how you interact with your family, your co-workers, fellow commuters, etc.?

Appointment with yourself

Designate "me" time on your calendar. Make appointments with yourself and then protect that time. Setting boundaries around your "me" time will make those days/hours/minutes non-negotiable. Be as committed to yourself as you are to others.

The following are what "me" time might include.

Listening to music, audiobooks, or podcasts

Reading a book

Taking a nap

Taking a walk or going on a nature hike

Exercising

Working on your own book or novel

Praying or meditating

Creating art or working on crafts

Wandering aimlessly

Going to a movie

Going to a museum

Spending time with friends

Watching your old favorite movies

Browsing at the library or your favorite bookstore

Taking a class that interests you

Doing nothing

Doing absolutely nothing

Thoughts on time

Saying yes to ourselves might mean saying no (or not now) to others. Helping others is great as long as you save enough energy to care for yourself. Granted, it may feel uncomfortable at first to say no to others, but it will get easier with practice.

Take some time for mindful consideration before agreeing to take on more responsibilities. If you are volunteering because you want to, that's wonderful! By all means keep doing it!

But if you're volunteering because you feel obligated or guilty, step back and decide if you want to continue down that path.

Are you willing to protect your "me" time even if it means saying *no* to others?

Don't let your yeses become your stresses.

Challenge — Make time for yourself

What are five things you would love to do if you had more time for yourself?

Of those five things, pick two that you will commit to doing once a day, once a week, or once a month for the next 90 days.

Write those two on your calendar now.

1. _____

2. _____

3. _____

4. _____

5. _____

When a calm state of mind is your starting point, chances are you will feel better prepared to handle life's detours and emergencies.

4

PLAN AHEAD

PLANNING AHEAD IS ONE WAY you can bring yourself to a more productive state. Can you plan for everything that may crop up in your day? Of course not, but, when you are organized in your home, in your office, in your life, and on your calendar, you will be better prepared to handle those unexpected events when they do crop up – and they will!

Calendaring

Daily

Assuming you use some kind of calendaring system, each night before you go to bed, take a couple of minutes to review your calendar. See what is scheduled for the next day and for the remainder of the week. You will know what is coming and hopefully this simple act of reviewing will decrease those frantic middle-of-the-night wake ups that you may be experiencing.

Weekly

Review your calendar on Sunday to prepare for the upcoming week. I review my calendar on Sunday afternoons. I send a quick email or text to confirm appointments, and I request recipients to respond *YES* to confirm. This has been highly effective in reducing last minute cancellations. For those who use a calendaring app, you can set these reminders to generate automatically.

Create a hub or command center

A *hub*, sometimes referred to as a *command center*, serves as the communication center in your home.

Ideally, a hub is located in a central location of the home. I've created them using underutilized pantries, kitchen nooks, extra bedrooms, dining rooms, laundry rooms, and even in a hall coat closet. You can even set up a small side table with a chair.

I have set up hubs for single people, roommates, busy families, multi-generational families, and retirees. Anyone can benefit from a hub!

A great addition to a hub is a bulletin board on which important paperwork like *To Do* lists, permission slips, outgoing mail, and the like can be pinned. (Inspirational quotes, happy notes, and fun photos can be posted there, too!)

The hub is also a great place for briefcases, purses, and backpacks to be emptied. Incoming mail can be sorted and processed here as well.

If you're comfortable with technology, this is an ideal place for a laptop or computer. Take advantage of the electronic calendaring systems that come with your email account. Those calendars can easily be shared, updated, and color coded for each person who has access.

The calendars can automatically be synced to your phones, too! A paper calendar is a great alternative if you're not comfortable going strictly digital.

A hub is an active center and should be kept purged and clutter-free.

Are you Proactive or Reactive with your time?

Having a good calendaring system that is up-to-date is the starting point for effective time management. However, we also need to look at how we prepare for and execute our calendar events.

I call this Proactive versus Reactive. Merriam Webster dictionary defines these words this way:

Proactive

  acting in anticipation of future problems, needs, or changes

Reactive

  a. readily responsive to a stimulus

  b. occurring as a result of stress or emotional upset

A proactive approach to life focuses on anticipating and/or eliminating problems before they arise. A reactive approach focuses on responding to events once they have occurred. *Working on becoming more proactive and less reactive will reduce stress in your life and help you protect "me" time on your calendar.*

Here's an example

If you are proactive, you may leave your house 10 minutes earlier than needed *just in case* there's a delay. You grab what you need and head out the door. You figure if you're a little early, that's fine because you will use those extra few minutes to catch up on some emails or read a few pages of that book you tucked under your arm as you walked out the door.

If you are reactionary, you may leave 10 minutes later than you need to. In a rush to get out the door, you may spill some coffee or have to run back in for something you forgot. *Ack, I'm going to be late!* Traffic delays or stopping for gas will add a little extra stress. The thought of arriving late may cause your heart to race. Off you go, zipping through traffic, and maybe even driving a little more aggressive than you know you should. If it all works out well, you arrive on time. Even if you're not late, you likely feel discombobulated and stressed.

In these scenarios, one is not right and the other wrong. As a community, we need people who plan and we need people who function well under stress. One is not better than the other.

But notice the stress levels in each scenario. If you are a person who wants to reduce the stress in your life, could you plan to leave five or ten minutes earlier than usual? Would that extra five or 10 minutes give you some breathing room?

What areas of your life cause you the most stress? Is it possible to take a proactive approach that might alleviate or reduce the impact of some of these stressors?

Caring for self

Chapter 3 was about making "me" time. Schedule time to care for yourself and do whatever it is that fills your cup and refuels your spirit. Please enter this time on your calendar and commit to practicing 30, 60, or 90 days. See what happens when you make yourself a priority. You may be pleasantly surprised at the positive results.

Are you willing to make plans that include self-care?

Caring for others

Dr. Phil McGraw is credited with saying, "We teach others how to treat us." If you believe that to be true, then teach people how to treat you well. Here are some suggestions for establishing healthy boundaries.

Enter appointments on your calendar for "me" time and don't cancel

Say "no" or "not now" when you want or need to

Stick to your guns (No means no, right?)

Those who have come to expect you to drop everything when they call or come over may be upset with you at first, but with calm conversation, consistency, and gentle reminding, they will come to accept this new behavior.

Ponder this

There is a reaction for every action. Saying yes to someone or something means you are saying no to someone or something else. Is that someone you?

Meals

For many, meal time is stressful and for others it is simply an afterthought. How often do you say, "I just realized I haven't eaten all day!" or "Darn, I forgot to take anything out for dinner *(again)*"?

Here are some tips to make meals a little easier.

Allocate time each week to

> Review your calendar for upcoming activities

> Plan a menu around those activities

> Create a grocery list

> Shop for groceries

> Prepare food for the upcoming week

Your menu does not have to be rigid but having one can certainly remove some stress from meal time. You won't continually be caught off-guard and operating in reactionary mode (which often leads to fast food and drive-thrus).

If you plan ahead and think creatively, you can easily create a couple of meals from one ingredient. Sunday night's leftovers might work well for Monday's lunch.

Combining errands

If you must go across town for an errand, determine if you have other errands you can do on the way or even in that same area of town. Combining errands saves time and saves money in fuel and unnecessary wear and tear on you and your vehicle. If you ride the bus or subway, combining errands saves time and fares, too!

Flexibility

Is planning the opposite of being flexible? No, it is not. Planning ahead does not mean being rigid. But, the better you plan, the more in control you feel, and the better you can adapt and flex when unexpected things occur.

It may sound strange, but planning may bring more spontaneity, flexibility, and joy to your life. You may find you have more time for hobbies or spur-of-the moment fun.

Challenge — 10 things you'll commit to doing

Write down 10 things that you know you need to do but have been ignoring (aka procrastinating). Tape the list to your computer, refrigerator, or bathroom mirror. You own this list. Read it mindfully every day.

Will you commit to completing your *To Do* list within the next 30, 60, or 90 days?

If you cannot realistically complete 100% of the items, can you complete 50%? 75%? More?

On your calendar, block time that allows you to start and finish each task. I suggest a start date and an end date for each item.

As you complete the *To Do* items, cross them off the posted list.

And remember, even little victories are cause for celebration!

	10 Things	Complete by (date)	Entered on calendar? ✓
1.			
2.			
3.			
4.			
5.			
6.			
7.			
8.			
9.			
10.			

If you save everything,
nothing is important.

5

LET GO OF EXCESS

A NYTHING IN YOUR SPACE OR ON YOUR CALENDAR that doesn't serve you well should be considered excess and subject to release.

Clutter can be overwhelming and stressful.

Clutter can be a physical manifestation of other issues.

Clutter can be embarrassing.

Clutter can cause feelings of guilt.

Clutter creeps.

Contained clutter is still clutter.

Clutter can be a health and safety hazard.

Clutter can keep you stuck in a home that no longer serves you well.

Clutter can come between relationships.

Letting go can be hard. Continuing to live in clutter is hard, too. If letting go of the excess and the chaos in your life can make room for some calm, the question is this:

Are you willing to do the work? Are you willing to make
the decisions that will free you from clutter?

There is no sugar-coating this; clearing clutter is work. It's a process; it takes focus and a lot of energy. Yet with your determination and the tools provided within these pages, you can free yourself from clutter.

If along the journey of turning chaos into calm you get stuck, simply pause. Refer back to this book, call in a family member or friend, or call a professional organizer. Just don't stop. Please, don't stop.

As mentioned throughout this book, you have to roll up your sleeves and take action. Identify problem areas, pick a project, plan ahead, schedule time, and jump in with both feet. Make decisions about what stays and what goes, and commit to starting AND completing your organizing projects.

Inaction breeds doubt and fear.
Action breeds confidence and courage.
Go out and get busy.
- Dale Carnegie

Time-appropriate tasks

WARNING: The process of getting organized often makes the space look worse than it did before you started. The last thing you want to do is create an even bigger mess and then leave it half-done.

Starting on a master closet when you only have an hour available is not advisable. Use that hour to work on a project you can reasonably expect to start *and* finish in that timeframe.

With very large projects, it is not realistic to expect that you will start and complete a project in one day. In those cases, decide on a clear stopping point.

For example, you can set the expectation of *I will purge and organize these three dresser drawers today. I will purge the next three drawers tomorrow. I will continue working on this dresser drawer project all week until it is completed.*

Minding your P's and Q's

People often ask, "How do I *stay* organized once I have completed a project?" I remind them that organized is not a project; organized is a lifestyle.

And then I share my *4P's for Success.* An organized lifestyle is the

Persistent,

Purposeful,

Purging, and

Placement of all that remains.

You see, organizing is never *done.* Every day offers more opportunities to receive more things into our space and to add more commitments to our calendar. The simplified life requires the application of the 4P's, over and over again.

Release all that no longer serves you

What no longer serves you could be possessions, people in your life, or even pressures on your time. Get clear about the things, the people, and the tasks that you are allowing in your life. Release anything that clutters your space, drains your energy, dampens your spirit, or wastes your time.

Let's be real here. At times, life pulls the rug out from under you and your time is not your own. We all have those occasions. Perhaps you are ill or are caring for an ill child or an aging parent. Maybe you've experienced a death in the family, a job loss, or a health scare.

These real-life situations can create havoc on your sense of calm and your progress towards simplifying life. During those difficult times, ask for help. You need calm now more than ever. For goodness sakes, take care of yourself.

Letting go of "just-in-case" items

Truth be told, we rarely need those *just-in-case* items and they are a big contributor to clutter. If you could replace the item easily and inexpensively, you have permission to let it go.

Here is a list of *just-in-case* items to consider releasing.

Worn out shoes

Old work clothes (unneeded uniforms, logoed clothing from previous jobs)

Out of style clothes

Clothes that no longer fit (too big or too small)

Excess empty jars and plastic containers

Used foil and baggies

Extra cords for unidentified electronics*

Old landline and office phone systems*

Old computer systems*

Old mobile phones*

Old medicine (dispose of responsibly)

Old bedsheets, bath towels, washcloths

Excess cleaning rags

*NOTE: Always use trustworthy sources when recycling electronics.

Nostalgic items

Making decisions on items that are nostalgic or hold emotional power can be difficult. For example, Grandmother's china, the dissertation from your Ph.D. program, clothes and toys from your children, or clothes from your own happier (or smaller) time.

TIP: When getting started with simplifying your life, leave the emotionally-charged projects for later. Start with less emotional stuff to build confidence and momentum.

Deciding what stays and what goes

To move through the process of simplifying your life and turning your chaos into calm, you have to make decisions about everything in your space. Apply the following four questions to everything you own. Your answers will determine whether items stay or go.

The Four Questions (4Q's)

Just as you need to address the 4P's, you have the 4Q's to ask yourself about your stuff.

1. Do I <u>LOVE</u> it?

2. Do I use it/wear it?

3. Does it serve me well?

4. Can it serve someone else better?

Let's begin with clothes

The *Toss, Keep, Out the door (TKO)* process was developed by Peter Walsh, author of several organizing books. It's simple and easy to remember.

Once you have answered the four questions, these are your choices.

1. Toss

Toss or recycle things that are too worn, too stained, non-repairable, etc. Place items in a bin, bag, or box appropriately labeled *Toss* or *Recycle*. (To reduce landfill impact, consider fiber and shoe recycling centers.)

2. Keep

Clothes – Remember, every item you keep needs a home. Hang clothes in a like-with-like manner and place them in the closet (I like to use velvet-lined hangers).

Like-with-like can mean shirts with shirts, pants with pants, or it can mean complete outfits hung together. Do what makes sense to you. Make a conscious effort to keep clothes hung where they belong.

Seasonal clothes - If your closet is stuffed to overflowing, moving heavy coats into a coat closet or extra bedroom closet will help. Place winter seasonal items such as gloves, mittens, and scarves in a bin or box and place them on a shelf when not in use. When winter comes, simply bring the bin down, put the items in drawers or hang them. Then place your summer clothes in the bin and return it to the top shelf.

Shoes – Store them in boxes, clear bins, or simply place them on shelves or cubbies. Heaping them on the floor is not a good solution. Separate by type. If you are pressed for space, place less frequently worn shoes on high, out of the way shelves. Take advantage of vertical space.

If you want to add another task to the project, take a photograph of the shoes, print it, and then affix it to the box or bin. This add-on task can be a time consuming project. Plan accordingly.

Remember, everything you keep must have a designated home. If you have too many things, go through the 4Q's process again. Keep purging until you find the comfort and space you seek.

3. Out the door

Set aside rejected items in a pile, bag, or box. These are things you wish to give away, donate, or sell.

These *Out the door* things need to leave your house as soon as possible. Load up your car and drop donations at your favorite charity the next time you're out. Or if you have too much to take yourself, schedule a pick up within the next week.

If you are holding on to items for someone to look through, give that person a deadline. You might say something like, "Come by this week. Anything that's left will be donated on Saturday."

I'm not sure

If you are really not sure on an item, set it aside for a couple of hours and then decide. You may find the decision to let go is much easier to make after you have decided on 1,000 other things. If you want to keep it, designate a home for it now.

Other options

Consignment stores often accept clothes, furniture, and other items. Many consignment stores require laundered and pressed clothes, and they want them brought in on hangers. Some consignment stores only accept clothes that are currently in season. They may also limit how many items you can consign and they may only accept your items on certain days or during certain hours. Be sure to check with your favorite consignment store to understand their policies. Request a receipt for any qualified tax donations.

Now you'll go through the same *Toss, Keep, Out the door* process and apply the 4Q's to your household goods.

Time Commitments

The 4Q's can also be applied to time commitments.

If you want to simplify your life and turn your chaos into calm you need to evaluate the commitments that take up your time. The following questions can be applied to your calendar.

1. Do I LOVE/ENJOY doing this?

2. Does doing this activity move me closer to or further away from my goals?

3. Does doing this activity serve me well?

4. Could someone else benefit from doing this job?

Your answers will help you decide if you are allocating your time based upon your values, priorities, and/or passions.

If your answers make you question your time commitments, consider re-evaluating how releasing some of those commitments might provide some relief and could help take back some of your precious time.

Give 'til it feels good, not 'til it hurts

Supporting causes that touch your heartstrings is certainly rewarding. Just be sure to reserve enough energy to properly care for yourself. As discussed earlier, it can be uncomfortable to say no, but it is also necessary at times. Remember, know your no.

No and *no thank you* are complete sentences. An explanation is not required unless you choose to do so. If you are already so busy that you are stressed out, and if your life is already filled with time commitments, saying no or no thank you is a reasonable response.

Know your no.

Challenge — Purge project

Closets

Will you commit to going through your closet and clearing out clothes you do not LOVE or WEAR?

If going through your entire closet seems overwhelming, will you commit to working through one side, or one shelf?

Or would you be willing to start with shoes? Purses? Hats? T-shirts?

Don't like that idea?

If the closet doesn't sound good to you, what other area of your home will you commit to purging and organizing? Kitchen? Garage? Office? Master bedroom? Storage unit?

It's time to get busy. It's time to let go of excess!

Ready, set, go!

Notes

_____

_____

_____

_____

_____

_____

_____

_____

_____

_____

_____

_____

_____

_____

_____

_____

_____

_____

Being organized has many benefits including saving time, saving money, and enhancing peace of mind.

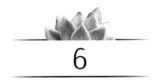

6

INVOLVE YOUR PEOPLE

I F YOU SHARE A HOME WITH OTHERS, getting them involved in the process of clearing clutter will be helpful. The challenge lies in the fact that we cannot control others. If you live with other people and they don't buy in to the *simplified life* concept, or are unwilling or unable to help, it will definitely be more difficult for you.

But what you can control is you. You can continue down your own path of turning chaos into calm.

So, even if you encounter resistance from others, you can still do something – even if it's a little something - to improve your own personal space. Be an example to others by organizing your own space, pick up after yourself, put things back where they belong, and finish what you start. Change your life and others may change theirs, too.

Case study

I once worked with a client whose spouse was resistant to her seeking outside help with her office. She had tried on numerous occasions to organize the area and to no avail. She told me she failed time and time again, and when she did try to get it cleared out and organized, she made an even bigger mess and got frustrated. She was overwhelmed and disappointed with herself.

To boot, her husband was not on board with her spending the money and he insisted she should be able to do it by herself. She replied that she really needed a professional's help and she would use money she had saved to hire one.

Her home office was in full view when entering the front door of the home. It was the *focal point* for guests who entered, and yes, it was a mess. She was ashamed and wanted the area to look nice and to also function well for her.

She had a successful business and she spent a lot of time in the office on the phone, meeting with clients, and networking. She didn't have time to waste looking for lost documents, and she desperately needed organizational systems that would simplify her life and turn her chaos into calm.

We sorted and purged paperwork, set up an efficient filing system, filed important papers, filled the recycle bin with outdated marketing materials, and shredded unneeded sensitive documents. We created a paper flow process for mail and incoming paperwork that she felt confident she could maintain. We organized her marketing materials and made it easy for her to *grab-and-go* as she was heading out the door to meetings.

No more showing up at meetings with outdated marketing materials for her! We set up a system for entering business cards into her computer, which also synced with her phone, so she would always have her client's contact information with her.

Once her home office was organized and functioning well, she was prepared to tackle other areas of her home on her own. She felt confident and empowered and now had the tools she needed to purge and organize the kitchen, pantry, and her sewing/craft room, all of which had been bothering her for years.

Here's where it gets interesting: After seeing his wife's progress, the resistant husband began purging and organizing his own stuff!

And this happened without her saying a word to him. He launched into his own organizing projects, and he started in the garage. In one weekend, he released four of the five sets of golf clubs, all the excess sporting equipment, and a lot of extra tools he no longer needed. He cleared shelves of outdated hardware, and household cleaning and car supplies. He was inspired to let go of the excess and simplify his life, and very likely his wife's successes led to that inspiration.

TIP: Clutter behaves like a virus, a bad virus. It takes over. Getting organized is like a virus, too - a GOOD virus. Organize one area in your home and you will likely want to organize and simplify other areas in your home, too.

Yours vs. Mine

Funny how often people think their stuff is more important than another person's stuff. A husband might see his partner's shoe collection as out of control and simply ridiculous. But when asked about his baseball cap collection or concert T-shirt collection from the 1970s, the tone magically shifts.

Blended families and multi-generational households deal with this quandary, too. In these cases, it is important to find a compromise that honors each person. Remember, we all have different tolerance levels for stuff in our space. Finding a suitable compromise is sometimes the best we can do.

Make your bed

Why? It's easy. It's doesn't take long. It looks nice. It sets the tone for a productive day. And you won't have to make it before you climb into it this evening (you know who you are).

SIDE NOTE: Check out the video of Naval Admiral William McRaven's address to graduating students at University of Texas at Austin in

> A bed with eight throw pillows is harder to make
> than a bed with two or three throw pillows.
> Keep it simple.

2014. You might be further inspired to make your bed. Here is a link to the speech: https://bit.ly/2xqVpNQ

A NOTE OF WARNING: If you do get help with a chore, refrain from criticizing, picking it apart, or "fixing" it, even if it's not up to your standards. If you criticize or fix it, for obvious reasons, your helper may just stop helping you.

If you live alone

You may have clutter that is all your own doing. That happens. If you want to simplify your life, you will go through all the same processes outlined throughout this book.

If you haven't already done so, reflect on how you got to this place – without judging. Think about how you want to live and use that vision as your focal point as you move forward.

If you are ready to change your current condition, move into action, and start on a time-appropriate project. You deserve it!

Remember, start small and think big.

Kids and clutter

Toys, clothes, and school paperwork are major sources of kids' clutter. The good thing is that when they are young, they "age out" of things, which means those things can be removed or released. You can box up these things and label them for the next child in line or you can give them away, sell them, or donate them.

The challenge is the very things that are no longer age-appropriate often become *"my favorite thing in the whole-wide world"* when it's time to let them go. Use the 4Q's as referenced in Chapter 5 to help you make decisions about what stays and what goes.

School paperwork flows in fast! From homework to permission slips to artwork. Process it daily. Consider setting up a box for your child's best work. At the end of the school year, go through and purge the box down to the really great pieces. At that point you may want to consider digitizing the paperwork and letting the originals go.

FUN TIP: Digitally photograph artwork and schoolwork and display those images on a digital frame or on a computer screen as a slideshow. How fun is that!

If you have more than one child, imagine if each child had their own digital frame. They could have a rotating slideshow of their best work and they could share it with others, too! What a wonderful way to honor their efforts and talent.

Photos and family history

Photographs hold memories, family history, and important stories. When people lose their homes to disasters, they usually say that they are just grateful to have survived. You might hear them say, "It's just stuff," or "We can rebuild." And then they add, "What we can't replace are the family pictures." In the midst of the chaos and heartbreak, they remember the photos.

The good news is that you can protect yourself against this devastating loss by digitizing your photos and family documents. If your family films, slides, photos, and negatives are packed into boxes or drawers or closets, do yourself and your family and future generations a favor by having them digitized.

You can find reputable companies to take your original photos, scan them, and save them onto electronic media and/or store them in the *cloud*. The company will typically return the originals to you. (Check their policy to ensure they meet your needs.)

You can then decide what to do with them. At that point, many people feel comfortable enough to let them go and they are willing to distribute them to loved ones, friends, libraries, or museums.

If you have damaged or discolored photographs, chances are you can have them repaired by companies that offer restoration service.

Where to start?

Gather all the photographs together and separate them into years. If you are able to take this step to the next level, separate them by year, then by month, and even by person. This is a time-consuming project that usually requires use of a large table. Plan accordingly.

Purge photos you don't want to digitize. This will save you time and it will save you money if you have them done professionally. Discard photos that are not of good quality (i.e., blurry, unrecognizable landscapes, people you do not recognize, people who are no longer significant, or are not part of the legacy you wish to pass on). If you have duplicate prints, discard one of them.

TIP: Keep the photos that tell the best stories. And then share those stories!

Digitizing

You can digitize photos yourself by using a high-quality setting on your scanner, or you can hire a service to digitize them for you. If you hire a service, inquire about backup and access options. Do your research and read the company's reviews. Ensure your photographs are protected and that you have access to them whenever you want them. Review company policies for returning originals to you.

File naming

If you are digitizing photos yourself, scan them using a high-quality setting and save them to your computer using a file naming convention that is consistent and relevant to you. Doing so will help you locate the photos on your computer with ease.

In the chart that follows, *Carl Jackson Photos* is the *umbrella* folder. All photos related to Carl Jackson will be saved into a *subfolder* or a *sub-subfolder*. Folder names should be descriptive; naming consistency is key.

Folder names can be edited at any point should you want to create something that is more meaningful to you.

This flowchart shows an example of the basic naming convention described above.

If this naming convention makes sense to you, great, use it! If not, create a naming sequence that does make sense to you, and then use it consistently.

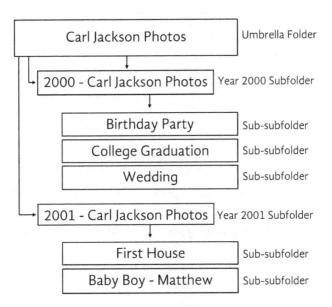

The goal is to be able to easily locate files on your computer. If you go to all the trouble to digitize your photos and then can't find them on your computer, what have you gained?

Backup your files

To prevent losing your files, it is imperative to regularly back up your computer. As a second layer of protection, consider backing up your computer to an external hard drive or to a cloud-based service.

8mm and film

Film can be digitized and many companies offer digitizing services for these media types. Or with the proper equipment, you can do it yourself.

Negatives and slides

Many scanners have the capability of digitizing negatives and slides. Digitizing companies also offer that service.

Letters, newspaper articles, certificates, etc.

Digitize letters, newspaper clippings, and certificates by scanning or having them scanned by a service. As a last resort, you can use a digital camera to take photos of the documents. Unless you are a pro, the quality is not normally as good as scanning, and lighting can be problematic.

Parental nostalgia

Parents' nostalgia goes something like this, "Aww, this outfit was so cute on Josey. I just can't give it away." This is not a problem unless every outfit carries that sentiment. Rather than saving every item of clothing the child ever wore, save a few of the special things and let the rest go.

Here's an idea

Consider creating a shadow box that commemorates that very special time. For example, you can frame the outfit the baby wore home from the hospital along with the wrist band and the birth announcement. Another idea for multiple pieces of clothing is to sew or commission a memory quilt, a quilted stuffed animal, or a doll using the fabric from those clothes.

Teaching organizational skills

Sure, some of us are hard wired for organization, but organization is a teachable skill.

From a young age, most children can recognize different shapes and colors. They are starting to understand the difference between a book and a ball.

When children have reached this level of maturity, with direction and interaction, many can start sorting using a like-with-like method. They can also start helping by putting things away.

This is where it is important to model good habits and to create easy organization systems. The easier the better. Remember, perfect is not the goal, and a good effort is cause for celebration!

The following list contains ideas where kids can help.

Hanging backpacks, coat, or jacket on hooks

Placing shoes in closet

Putting toys in toy box or bins

Placing books on bookshelves

Hanging wet bath towels on hooks

Placing dirty clothes in hamper

Helping sort laundry (by color, by type)

Helping put laundry in drawers

Pulling covers up on the bed

Clearing plates from the table

Separating silverware

Clothes

Having too many clothes can make it difficult to decide what to wear. This applies to kids as well as adults. Having too many clothes means laundry can pile up for weeks before it *has* to be done. Clothes can become a battlefield between parents and kids and it doesn't have to be that way. Help your children simplify their lives, too.

Spend some time with your child(ren) on Sunday evening picking out clothes for the upcoming week. These outfits can be folded together and placed neatly in a drawer, on a shelf, or in a hanging closet organizer that has slots for each day of the week.

Toys and Games

Children outgrow toys just like they outgrow clothes. Purge often.

Grandparents

Grandparents are often guilty of giving too much to their grandchildren. If this is the case in your family, it might be time to have "the talk." If clean up time has become a battlefield or is too much work, explain how the excessive toys, gifts, and clothes are causing a lot of stress for your child and for you.

For holidays or birthdays, you might see if the grandparents would like to go in on one big gift with you instead of a bunch of little gifts. Or perhaps they could give the gift of experience like a membership, museum passes, or a trip to Disneyland. Educational or extracurricular funding is another option. Experiences do not add clutter and that, in and of itself, simplifies life.

Challenge — 10 things per day
(a 5-day exercise in letting go)

Walk around your home or office and gather 10 things you are willing to let go of <u>today</u>.

If you need help deciding what to release, apply the 4Q's.

Do I <u>LOVE</u> it?

Do I use/wear it?

Does it serve me well?

Can it serve someone else better?

Place those 10 things in a box or in a designated spot for disposal at the end of the week.

Repeat this challenge for five days and you will have released 50 things. Do it for 10 days and you will have released 100 things!

You are simplifying your life. You are turning chaos into calm!

If you live with other people or know others who would benefit from this challenge, invite them to join you. Share your progress and celebrate your victories.

Be sure to join our support group,
SOS Clutter Disruptors on Facebook.

Refusing to ask for help when you need it is refusing someone a chance to be helpful.
- Ric Ocasek

7

FIND HELP

PERHAPS YOU HAVE TRIED TO GET ORGANIZED BEFORE. Perhaps you have even hired a professional organizer. If you are reading this book, chances are you have other organizing books, too. It's highly likely you have cut out a few *How to Organize Your* _____ *(fill in the blank)* articles from magazines or newspapers, or maybe you even belong to an online group and you receive *Clutter Challenges* or tips on getting organized.

All that is just more clutter unless you apply the principles within this book. You have to do the work. Reading about it is not going to fix the problem.

If you have not done any of the challenges in this book, ask yourself why. Maybe you've started organizing projects in the past, and even completed a few, but here you are again, unorganized and quite possibly overwhelmed.

If you have tried and can't seem to get it done, understand you are not alone. Organization can be very challenging for some. Just know, if you really want to simplify your life and turn your chaos into calm, help is available when you're ready to accept it.

Address underlying issues

If you have an underlying medical or emotional issue that is complicating your progress, seek help from a physician or counselor.

Simplifying your life, reducing your stress, and giving yourself some breathing room will likely complement your treatment plan.

Who can help me?

If you are physically unable to do the work, ask for help. If you just cannot get started or if you perpetually start but do not finish organizing projects, get some help. Call a trusted family member, call a friend, or hire a professional organizer.

Neutral party

While well-meaning, sometimes family and friends are not the best choice to help you with your organizing projects. Not because they are bad people, but because your relationship is different than working with a neutral party.

As you go through the decluttering and simplifying process, you might be dealing with emotionally-charged things and in many cases, sensitive information. Make sure you feel comfortable and confident that the person you invite in is the right one for you.

Professional organizers

If you decide to work with a professional organizer, seek out one who has proven experience. Do your research because organizers don't need licensure to use the title. Do an Internet search or ask friends, family, or colleagues if they can recommend an organizer. And then review the organizer's website and read reviews, search for him/her on LinkedIn and read the recommendations, find him/her on social media and read his/her posts. If you like what you see, make contact with the organizer.

The National Association of Productivity & Organizing Professionals (NAPO) website (www.napo.net) is another place to search for an organizer. Professional organizers aren't required to belong to NAPO, but those of us who do, subscribe to a code of ethics.

The first code states: *I will serve my clients with integrity, competence, and objectivity, and will treat them with respect and courtesy.* NAPO-affiliated professional organizers also have access to advanced curriculum and expanded business connections.

Referrals

An organizer may not be able to help you, and it could be for any number of reasons. Sometimes it is simply a matter of work load, distance, size of the project, or a deadline challenge. The organizer may offer a referral to another organizer or provide other resources that can better meet your needs.

There are no secrets to organization.

There are no shortcuts either.

There is work and a commitment to change the behaviors that got you here in the first place.

8

YOU CAN DO IT!

THIS IS WHERE THE RUBBER MEETS THE ROAD. If you have not already started purging, clearing clutter, organizing your space, evaluating relationships, and reviewing commitments on your time, it's time to start. Go back and review the challenges (look for the bullseye targets) and do a few of them. It is time to implement what you have learned from this book.

You have everything you need *right now* to simplify your life and turn your chaos into calm.

During the simplifying process, please don't strive for perfection - from yourself or from others. That's too much pressure. If you set your standards too high, you'll create unnecessary stress.

And remember, criticizing another's attempts at getting organized can create resistance or, worse yet, can stop the project dead in its tracks. If you want participation and help from others, release the mindset that says, "If I want it done right, I have to do it myself."

The less is more mindset

The more stuff you have, the more stuff you have to put away, clean, launder, dust, and manage.

Is simplifying life easy? Not necessarily. In fact, it might be hard. But the effort required to create the life you want will be well worth it.

Imagine living a less stressed life.

Imagine walking into your home and loving it.

Imagine walking into your closet and loving everything that's in there.

Imagine being able to find things when you need them.

Imagine a day or week that includes some "me" time.

Imagine having the freedom to do more of the things you enjoy.

Imagine a life that isn't burdened with every weekend allocated to household chores.

No need to imagine these things.

Simplify your life and turn your chaos into calm.

Less *is* more.

Mindfulness

Many people are creatures of habit. Problems with disorganization, clutter, and chaos tend to appear in the same places over and over. Be mindful of your tendencies and your habits. When things start accumulating or you find yourself backsliding into old habits, stop! Spend some time cleaning up the clutter before it gets out of hand. Remember, clutter is like a virus and it will spread if you don't take care of it in a timely manner.

The news

Clutter and chaos go hand-in-hand and you can't wish it away. The clutter is here and it has to be dealt with. Spending time in guilt over money spent, chores not done, and uncompleted projects will only drag you down.

As the saying goes, "Stop looking in the rearview mirror; you're not going that way." Be present and get to work.

With every project, you will start right where you are. Take one step forward every day. Each step you take will be an important part of your progress. On days when you fall backwards, vow to start again. That's it, just start again. Simplifying life and turning chaos into calm is a journey and quitting is not an option.

The good news

You are still reading this book and by now, you have probably contemplated or even started and hopefully completed some of the challenges from previous chapters. If you have done some purging and organizing, congratulations! You *are* moving forward, and you *are* improving your current condition.

If you haven't done any of the challenges or haven't asked for help, ask yourself why? What's keeping you stuck? What's holding you back? What or who is in your way? Can you put your head down and just bust through those things?

The great news

Professional help is available if you need help clearing clutter, creating organizational systems, and simplifying your life. A professional organizer can help navigate the clutter, provide guidance, and lessen the time it takes to complete projects.

Focus on the benefits

Getting organized can be hard work and when you are tired or frustrated, it's helpful to focus on the benefits. Getting organized can save you money, save you time, and should enhance your peace of mind.

How, you ask?

Money benefits of getting organized

- ► Reduces or eliminates duplicate purchases (because you know what you have)

- ► Reduces or eliminates overbuying (because you make mindful purchases)

- ► Reduces eating out (because you have a meal plan)

- ► Reduces spoiled fruit and vegetables (because you have done meal prep)

- ► Reduces expired food (because you keep your pantry and cupboards organized)

Time benefits of getting organized

- ► Less time spent searching for lost items (because everything has a place)

- ► Less time spent shopping for things you already have (because you know what you have)

- ► Less time cleaning (because you have less stuff)

- ► Less time running errands (because you now combine errands)

Peace of Mind benefits of getting organized

Less stress

Less stress

Less stress

Congratulations! You have successfully simplified your life and have turned your chaos into calm.

Change happens when the pain of staying the same is greater than the pain of change.
- Tony Robbins

MAINTENANCE

THROUGH NORMAL LIVING, new things will continue to creep into your space. It could be because of your purchases, gifts, holidays, moving to a new place, adding family members, empty-nesting, downsizing, inheritances from others, life transitions, or a combination of the above.

Events and life changes are part of living. Just be careful of *clutter creep.* Follow up is crucial to maintain the order you've worked so hard to create. Revisit this book when you notice things start piling up again, and apply the principles you've learned. Remember, start small, think big.

Next steps

Once you have purged and organized your space, a deep cleaning is a good idea. This might be a great time to have your carpets shampooed and your windows and blinds cleaned, too.

Many professional organizers work closely with people in the cleaning trades and can give you the names of a few reputable companies. As with hiring anyone, do your research.

The key to staying organized is maintenance. You'll recall Chapter 5's explanation of the 4P's Persistent, Purposeful, Purging, and Placement of all that remains. Being organized is a lifestyle, not a project.

Self-assessment

Think about where you were before you started this book. Do you feel better equipped to simplify your life? Are you going to do the work yourself or is it time to call in help?

Have you already taken necessary steps to start and complete projects? If you took Before and After photos of your projects, now is a great time to look at them again. A celebration is probably in order!

It doesn't matter where you are coming from.
All that matters is where you are going.
- Brian Tracy

SWEET SIMPLICITY

LIVING A SIMPLER AND MORE INTENTIONAL LIFE is within your reach. You read this book, which leads me to believe you desire less chaos and more calm. You want to *Simplify Your Life*. You want to *Turn Your Chaos into Calm*, and now you have the tools to do so.

As you move forward, remember to focus on the goal of living a simpler life, and take one step at a time, one day at a time. A simplified life has no quick fixes; no magic. But if you will stick with it, a simpler, calmer and more peaceful existence can be yours.

If you get stuck or lose interest, visualize your goal. Remember, you do not have to imagine anymore. It's yours for the taking.

"When we adopt a life of sweet simplicity, peace and calm will prevail. Not every day, but certainly more days than not."

Here's to peace.

Here's to calm.

Here's to you.

INSPIRATIONAL QUOTES
(All quotes written by Andrea Brundage)

Getting organized is the process. Living organized is a lifestyle.

Being organized has many benefits, including saving time, saving money, and enhancing peace of mind.

If we save everything, nothing is important.

When overwhelmed about where to begin, pick a corner and work your way out.

There is no magic to tidying up. There is hard work built on desiring improvement of the current situation, developing organizational systems that work with your life flow, and committing to follow through consistently, thus creating new habits.

Free up that cluttered space so you can breathe! Breathing is important.

Do not be blinded by a perceived good deal. Three for $1 is not a good deal if what you purchase goes to waste.

Do not make financial decisions or long-term commitments (one year or longer) when you are in a highly stressed or emotionally fragile state.

Home should be your sanctuary. From the moment you step over the threshold, you should feel safe and welcomed.

When taking on any large organizing project, the space will look worse before it looks better.

When you are unable to start and complete a project in one day, tidy up as best you can and get back to work on it tomorrow.

What if we called it "right-sizing" instead of downsizing? Ah, yes, that feels better, doesn't it?

There is a reaction for every action. Saying yes to someone or something means you are saying no to someone or something else.

If you are serious about simplifying, you must start with purposeful purging.

MOTIVATION

SEEK OUT MOTIVATION wherever and whenever you can. Jot down quotes that inspire you, read authors whose words resonate with you, journal, and watch videos that make you feel motivated. These are all tools that can provide motivation as you continue on the journey to *Simplify Your Life*.

The following are some well-known holidays along with some fun off-the-wall ones that may offer inspiration.

January Motivation

New Year's Day

Get Organized (GO) Month

National Clean Out Your Closets Month

National Clean Off Your Desk Day (2nd Monday of January)

National Clean Up Your Computer Month

National Clean Out Your Inbox Week (last week in January)

National Financial Wellness Month

International Quality of Life Month

International Data Privacy Day (January 28)

February Motivation

National Archive Your Files Month

National Time Management Month

Declutter for a Cause Month

Clean Out Your Computer Day (2nd Monday in February)

Valentine's Day (February 14)

Random Acts of Kindness Day (February 17)

International Expect Success Month

National Plant the Seeds of Greatness Month

MARCH MOTIVATION

National Organize Your Home Office Day (2nd Tuesday in March)

National Clean Up Your IRS Act Month (get ready for taxes)

National Craft Month

Procrastination Week (1st full week of March...are you sure you want to participate in this?)

Optimism Month

National Clean Out Your Closet Week (3rd week in March)

National Clutter Awareness Week (4th week in March)

World Backup Day (March 31...backup those electronic files!)

APRIL MOTIVATION

Stress-Awareness Month

National Organize Your Files Week (3rd full week in April)

National Records & Information Management Month

Tax Day (April 15)

International Earth Day (April 22)

National TV-Free Week (4th week in April)

National Decorating Month

National Car Care Month

MAY MOTIVATION

National Moving Month

National Small Business Month (2nd week in May)

Mother's Day (2nd Sunday in May)

Older Americans Month

World History Day/International Day of the Families (May 15)

National Photography Month (organize those photos)

National Scrapbooking Day (1st Saturday in May)

National Scrapbooking Month

Memorial Day

June Motivation

National Garage & Storage Organizing Month

National Email Week (clean up those emails)

Let It Go Day (June 23)

National Safety Month

National World Environment Day (June 5)

Father's Day (3rd Sunday in June)

JULY MOTIVATION

National Financial Freedom Day (July 1)

Workaholic Day (July 5)

National Give Something Away Day (July 15)

Make a Difference to Children Month

AUGUST MOTIVATION

National Simplify Your Life Week (1st week in August)

National Garage Sale Day (2nd Saturday in August)

Happiness Happens Month

What Will Be Your Legacy Month

National Safe At Home Week (last week in August)

National Thrift Shop Day (August 17)

Mail Order Catalog Day (August 18)

Back to School

September Motivation

National Preparedness Month

Attention Deficit Hyperactivity Disorder Month

National Self-Improvement Month

Fight Procrastination Day (September 6)

National Coupon Month

Labor Day

Hunger Action Month

Swap Ideas Day (September 10)

National Grandparents Day (September 13)

World Gratitude Day (September 21)

October Motivation

National Home-Based Business Week (2nd week in October)

National Estate Planning Awareness Week (3rd week in October)

Organize Your Medical Information Month

National Book Month

National Depression Education & Awareness Month

National Kitchen & Bath Month

Positive Attitude Month

Work & Family Month

National Family History Month

Take Back Your Time Day (October 24)

Make A Difference Day (4th Saturday in October)

November Motivation

National Fraud Awareness Week (3rd week in November)

National Pursuit of Happiness Week (2nd week in November)

National Clean Out Your Refrigerator Day (November 15)

National America Recycles Day (November 15)

National Buy Nothing Day (day after Thanksgiving)

National Computer Security Day (November 30)

December Motivation

National Stress-Free Holidays Month

National Make Up Your Mind Day (December 31)

RESOURCES

Andrea Brundage can be reached at
info@AndreaBrundage.com

Facebook support group: *SOS Clutter Disruptors*

This group was created to provide support to anyone on the *Simplify Your Life* journey. Hope you will join us!

Feng Shui

An ancient Chinese philosophy whose literal translation to English is wind-water. This practice governs spatial arrangement and orientation in relation to the flow of energy and balance. Feng Shui practitioners are often sought out to help with design, furniture placement, and the implementation of remedies to clear blocked energy.

KonMari Method of Organizing

This method of organizing was developed by Marie Kondo and it has recently gained popularity. Kondo's basic philosophy asks the reader to ask themselves, "*Does this* (whatever it is) *spark joy*?" If it doesn't, it gets released.

Minimalism and the 90/90 Rule

A methodology for decluttering that asks two basic questions: *"Have I used this in the last 90 days? Will I use this in the next 90 days?"* If the answer is no, it goes. This process has been made popular by Joshua Fields Millburn and Ryan Nicodemus (aka *The Minimalists*).

Reading

Feng Shui Simplified by Sharyn Jordan Hathcock (aka The Home Whisperer). Decluttering is a very important feng shui principle and the reasons why it is important are covered in this book. This is a fun book with exercises you can apply in your own home and office to increase flow and release "stuck" energy.

One Simple Thing by Dr. Mallary Tytel. This is an excellent book that reminds us that one simple thing can change everything. The book asks you to do *one simple thing* every day and in so doing, you will discover who you are, and what is most important to you. The book includes an extensive list of ideas for simple things you can do each day.

Essentials: Essays by the Minimalists by Joshua Fields and Ryan Nicodemus. This is a collection of stories from the authors about minimalism and intentional living. Additionally, their 2016 film, *Minimalism: A Documentary,* examines and explains minimalism and offers stories from people who have chosen the minimalist lifestyle.

The Life-Changing Magic of Tidying Up by Marie Kondo. This book has led many to question everything in their space and to identify and keep only things that "spark joy." Many people say this book changed their thinking in very profound ways.

ABOUT THE AUTHOR

ANDREA BRUNDAGE IS AN EXPERIENCED PROFESSIONAL ORGANIZER who was blessed with the gift of organizing. She feels fortunate to work in a profession that aligns her gifts with her passion for helping others.

She had a long corporate career, holding management roles in office administration and accounting. She founded Simple Organized Solutions, LLC in Arizona in 2003 while working full-time, raising a family, and working towards her MBA degree.

Andrea has helped hundreds of clients with organizational projects in homes and corporate offices, and she has spoken to thousands on the topic of organization, downsizing, time management, and work-life balance.

She is frequently interviewed as an expert organizer and has been quoted by several nationally recognized online sites such as *BBC-Online, MSN Finance, Yahoo Finance, NPR* radio and others, and her guest articles can be found in a variety of magazines. She has also appeared as the expert organizer on several local television programs.

Simplify Your Life: 8 Simple Principles to Turn Your Chaos into Calm is Andrea's first book.

You can reach Andrea at
info@AndreaBrundage.com